SaaS Startup for Beginners

The most easiest Startup integration for getting Funding

Vardhane Harsh
Thanks to SaaSmetrics

www.vardhaneharsh.com

email- consulting@vardhaneharsh.com

This book is a compilation of what I've learned about managing SaaS Startups - particularly about how dealing with subscription metrics can mean the difference between the success and failure for your business.

Index

Introduction

Day and Night you guys work on your innovative ideas to give them a shape of a successful Startup. Of Course the main hurdle you would be facing is funding.SaaS integration can help you a lot for getting that seed you think you deserve.Let me enlighten you on SaaS.

There's an interesting fact behind business metrics: the more you use them, the more data-driven you become. I'm not saying you shouldn't listen to your heart and distrust your intuitions as an entrepreneur or manager, but one thing is true – once you truly tame your numbers you'll never want to play without them again.

Entrepreneurs have no trouble on building awesome products, many however don't know how to take their business to the next level. Clearly one of the ways of doing that is to have the skills and the discipline necessary to collect and analyze the relevant business data.

Running a subscription business radically changes your focus to monetizing long-term customer relationships. Businesses need to recognize that pricing, order management, metrics, financials and revenue all need to be handled differently in this new business model.

If you're just looking at today's revenues, you're in for some nasty surprises. Churn, lifetime value, monthly recurring revenue (MRR), and Customer Acquisition Cost are leading indicators of later revenues and core metrics at the subscription economy.

Welcome to the subscription economy

The term "subscription economy" refers to the business of offering subscriptions to consumers. For some startups, their entire business relies on a subscription business model. Examples of these include Netflix, Spotify, Zipcar, and all SaaS startups such as Salesforce and HubSpot.

It's actually not that new: the subscription business model has been around since our great-grandparents had their milk delivered to their door, but over the last two decades it has been increasingly adopted by technology and media startups. Businesses have been selling monthly subscriptions for all sorts of goods and services, offering anything from online software to food for a flat monthly fee.

Subscription is rapidly becoming the default business model for any company looking to accelerate growth, maximize cash, and increase its value. Currently, there is an increase in subscription startups as part of a larger shift from the product economy to the subscription economy. Businesses need to handle customer loyalty, pricing, and selling differently.

Why subscription business is different?

Running a subscription company means there is a continuing relationship with the customer. No longer does the business-customer relationship end with the swipe of a credit card.

Once you acquire a new customer you have recurring revenue,

which means you don't have to worry about one-off sales every month. Different from traditional sales, it gives you new challenges such as retention and churn.

One-time sales	Subscription
The booking is everything	The booking is the beginning
Fewer moving parts	More moving parts
Sales performance driven P&L	Model driven P&L
Less visibility/predictability	More predictability
Fast-moving levers	Slow building business

Complexity

On a subscription business there are more moving parts to every transaction. You're looking for long-term contracts and commitments. You can't just persuade a customer to buy something, knowing that we'll get upset or feel betrayed and leave you the next day. Complexity perpetuates and builds.

Visibility

Internally, you can see far into the future – and external readers can't see as much as they'd like. P&L is also more indicative of fundamental structure than of quarterly performance.

Speed

Business builds slowly – and sometimes expensively – over time.

Subscription business demands patience, no fix is quick. Actions you take today will have effect months or years later.

Subscription business brings additional stress on finance teams and financial systems to provide the visibility for long-lead-time decision making, as well as to manage the complexity as the business grows.

A new customer behavior

Today, many powerful business platforms are easily accessible. In many cases, business users can get a 30-day free trial by simply sharing their email address. That's a pretty low-risk requirement for a business buyer to check out a platform that could save them time and money on the job, help them collaborate better with teammates or create some impressive charts or graphs to add value to their next business initiative.

If a product provides value for today's B2B market, a "tryer" will become a "buyer" by utilizing the platform on a trial basis with a current work project or initiative. If your product successfully adds value to a current initiative, that value will become associated with your company and your products.

Many subscription economy startups base their sales strategy on ways they can acquire the masses. By design, their strategy is to continuously provide more "free access" to increase usage, embed information, establish value and build loyalty. If done well, at some point, users of your "freemium model" are going to want to collaborate on projects with others, share more information and have more security controls.

That's when it happens. Your tryers officially become buyers. They raise their hands and cross the threshold into the world of a paying customer.

The shift to subscription

Last year, Adobe decided to move its software suite for creatives to the cloud. The transition was far from perfect, but the results have mostly been positive. The company says 20% of customers that are purchasing the updated online tools weren't Adobe customers before the switch. And now that the software is cloud-based, Adobe can better track how customers are using it and constantly push updates to individual users.

Most of the complaints primarily seem to be coming from users who don't wish to have every upgrade, or those who don't need an entire suite of apps. However, Adobe's managed to move over 500,000 cloud subscriptions in just under a year, so they've decided to ignore that hue and cry.

On the other hand users says many of the new upgrades are too good to resist, and spreading out the pain over time let them invest the bucks elsewhere – like the inevitable hardware updates required to keep such software running smoothly.

Other startups who have made the switch have found they're able to attract a broader customer base by offering a subscription-based model, which has a much lower upfront cost to consumers. But the transition is sometimes easier on the customer than on the company, where the transformation to a new business model can be incredibly disruptive to the way sales and marketing is run.

Why should your company consider it?

Paying customers means recurring revenue for your company, and it's a driving factor behind a company's decision to decide for the subscription model. It helps startups maintain profitability and make informed decisions about future operational initiatives, creating what Aaron Ross calls predictable revenue.

In the subscription model, sales process decisions are more likely to be focused on "buyer first," versus the "product first" approach of traditional models. Internal conversations focus more on customer success metrics determined by changes in your customer acquisition cost, changes in your customer lifetime value and your success rate in upselling a percentage of your accounts to a premium product or service model.

This new approach requires a very different way of looking at your sales process and your overall business model. The luxury of having more predictability in your business model comes with some caveats: (1) the responsibility of successfully navigating scores of customer interactions and (2) the inherent risk that each interaction will either strengthen or weaken your customer experience.

Transitioning to or enabling integration of a subscription-based sales model will fundamentally change the way you operate your business. It will also affect many key functional areas of the organization.

History shows us that it worth the shot, and the present says that's the future ahead of us. Are you ready to make the shift?

Recurring revenue

Recurring revenue is simply the portion of a company's revenue that is highly likely to continue in the future. This is revenue that is predictable, stable and can be counted on in the future with a high degree of certainty.

Recurring revenue streams are usually based on a subscription business model. It's common to use monthly and annually subscriptions – but the period may vary according to the business characteristics and its consumers.

According to John Warrillow, the author of the book *"Built do Sell"*, there are few things more important than recurring revenue for a business owner who is prepping to sell a company. Recurring revenue is predictable revenue that can be expected to continue in the future.

Warrillow ranked the six different types of recurring revenue, described on the list below:

Hard contracts

What's the holy grail of recurring revenue? Look no further than your cell phone contract. "When the iPhone launched in the United States, AT&T insisted that you buy a three-year contract. Why? Because the stock value of AT&T mobile went up and down based on that contract revenue," Warrillow says.

Auto renewal subscriptions

Even better than these two subscription models are the kinds of subscriptions that go on forever, or at least until a customer tells it to stop. In the world of recurring revenue this is known as an "evergreen." Document storage subscriptions are good examples of evergreens.

Sunk money subscriptions

A sunk money subscription requires the initial purchase of a platform or product. A good example of this is the Amazon Kindle – that requires you to buy the e-reader in order to subscribe to Kindle Unlimited read-all-you-want e-book subscription.

Straight-up subscriptions

These are finite subscriptions, like for magazines that offer an optional re-up period at the end of the contract.

Sunk money consumables

This is when a customer makes an initial investment in a platform. For example, what if instead of going to Starbucks, you prefer to make your own coffee at home, and purchase a $300 Nespresso coffee maker to prepare hundreds of cups over the long haul.

Now you need to buy the capsules to make it work. This means that as a consumer, you've bought a platform rather than just a product. In the world of recurring revenue, platforms trump products every day of the week.

Are you desperate for a grande, three-pump cinnamon dolce, soy, no whip, no foam latte? Or maybe just a drip coffee? Either way, if you're a loyal Starbucks customer you're coming back for more of the company's products.

Of course some models are better than others, and we don't want customers to stay around because they're tied to a contract, but because they actually can't live without our product or service.

Subscriptions business with recurring revenue operates in a way that is fundamentally different than traditional business. Customers are the center of a subscription business, so key metrics are more often about customers than products.

Because the subscription economy is built on long-term customer relationships, the longer and stronger you can build these relationships, the more successful you'll be.

What makes recurring revenue so valuable is that you can spend more of your energy growing your business rather than on trying to acquire enough new or repeat business just to hit the same revenue level you did the year before.

CHAPTER 2
Data-driven

It's clear that embracing existing data is the most accurate, scalable and cost-effective solution for the subscription economy.

Unfortunately, most startups lack the advanced data integration capabilities needed to make it possible. For many, data is captured and stored across many different platforms and applications, making it almost impossible to gather and manage data that is constantly shifting.

Even harder, is to know exactly what to do with the data.

A business metric is a quantifiable measure that is used to track and assess the status of a specific business process. It's important to note that business metrics should be employed to address key audiences surrounding a business, such as investors, customers and different types of employees, such as executives.

Every area of business has specific metrics that should be monitored – marketers track campaign and program statistics, sales teams monitor new opportunities and leads, and executives look at big picture financial metrics.

SaaS and subscription businesses are more complex than traditional businesses. Traditional business metrics totally fail to capture the key factors that drive SaaS performance.

In the SaaS world, there are a few key variables that make a big difference to future results. This section of the book is aimed at helping subscription professionals understand which variables really matter, and how to measure them and act on the results.

As you can imagine, there are hundreds of different metrics that can be measured in a subscription business, and that's only considering the standards. If you sum up your own specific metrics - like product usage - the number of things to keep track gets insanely high.

The right thing to do is to focus on specific metrics according to the stage of your company. You don't want to start a startup on your garage and measure EBITA from day one, right?

The right metrics for each stage of your SaaS business

For a subscription business, there are a few key metrics that need your undivided attention. And the priority of these metrics shift as you grow.

This means that instead of measuring dozens or hundreds of different metrics, you should start with the core only and evolve from there – as your business grows and demands more control and higher complexity.

The following guideline will help you:

- By focusing only on the key metrics, you'll also be focusing on the core problems you need to solve to get your business to the next level;

- Data doesn't do you any good unless you act on it. Each of these metrics clearly tells you how you're doing. Right away, you'll know where you need to spend your time;

- Each stage complements the previous one with more comprehensive and complex metrics. You probably want to add (not remove) metrics along the way.

Super Early Stage Startups	Qualitative Feedback
	Customer Engagement
	Website Visits, Leads & Conversion

Early Stage Startups	All the above, plus:
	Bookings
	Monthly & Annual Recurring Revenue
	Customer Count
	Gross Churn
	Average Revenue per Account
	Customer Acquisition Cost
	Customer Lifetime Value
	LTV:CAC Ratio
	Up-front Invoicing
	Cash

Growth Stage Startups	All the above, plus:
	Net Churn
	Up-sell, Cross-sell & Down-sell
	Gross Margin
	Cost of Goods Sold
	Cohort Analysis
	Expenses
	Forecasted Sales & Quota
	EBITDA
	YoY, MoM Customers & Revenue Growth
Public Startups	All the above, plus:
	Deferred Revenue
	Market Penetration
	Segmentation & Exploratory Analysis

Metrics are limitless. You can segment and cross-reference almost any data point, such as customers by region, size, industry – revenue, customers and churn growth month-over-month, year-over-year and etc. There are hundreds if not thousands of possible combinations.

But be careful: there's a thin line between not going deep enough and over-measuring your business numbers.

What we're going to see in the next chapter is an overview of the most important metrics for any subscription business, but keep in mind that it's up to you to decide what should be measured.

CHAPTER 3
SaaS Metrics

The list below describes the definition, characteristics and formulas of some core SaaS and subscription metrics. We're focusing on 6 key metrics that are probably the most important of all – no matter your company's stage.

There are different ways to calculate each one of them. We're presenting the most accepted and well-know formulas – but it's ok if you do it differently.

Monthly Recurring Revenue MRR

What is MRR?

Monthly Recurring Revenue, almost always referred as MRR, is probably the most important metric at all of any subscription business. It's what makes this business model so great.

The general concept is that MRR is a measure of the predicable and recurring revenue components of your subscription business. It will typically exclude one-time and variable fees, but for month-to-month businesses could include such items.

As the names says, MRR represents recurring revenue on a monthly basis, but it could me measured as ARR (Annual Run Rate), which is simply MRR * 12.

How to calculate MRR?

The better way of doing it is to simply sum the monthly fee paid by every single customer. Let's say you have *Customer A* paying $200/mo and *Customer B* paying $100/mo. Your MRR would be $300.

See that each customer may be paying a different amount of money - since you can have different plans or event different products in your portfolio.

MRR = SUM (Paying customers monthly fee)

Average revenue per account

An easier way to calculate it is using the ARPA. Once you know the average revenue per account - some times called ARPU (average revenue per user) - all you should do is multiply the total number of paying customers by the average revenue each customer is bringing in. So let's say you have 10 paying customers and an average amount of $100/mo, your MRR would be $1,000.

MRR = ARPA * Total # of Customers

How to calculate MRR growth?

You might think that if you acquire more customers you MRR would grow, right? That's true, but not the only aspect to be considered on a subscription business model. To analyze MRR - and specially MRR growth - we should consider three different aspects of MRR:

New MRR

New MRR is the simply new revenue brought by newly customers acquired. So let's say you have acquired on a given month 5 new customers paying $100/mo and 2 new customers $200/mo. Your New MRR for that month would be $900.

Expansion MRR

Now image that you have 3 customers that upgrade their plans from $100/mo to $200/mo. That means you have expanded your revenue from existing customers, we call that Expansion MRR. Your Expansion MRR for that month would be $300.

Keep in mind that Expansion MRR can come from upselling (customers upgrading theirs plans) or cross-selling (customers buying additional products or services).

Churned MRR

And you should also consider churn. Churned MRR is the revenue that has been lost from customers cancelling or downgrading their plans.

So let's say on a given month you had 2 cancellations of $100/mo plans and other 3 customers downgraded their plans from $200/mo to $100/mo. You Churned MRR would be $500.

It simply means that you'll have minus $500 on recurring revenue for next month. Keep in mind that MRR churn is different from customer churn.

MRR Growth

Finally, to calculate your MRR growth you should actually consider all these three aspects on a formula.

Net New MRR = New MRR + Expansion MRR - Churned MRR

What about annual plans?

If you don't bill on a monthly basis, you should normalize your revenue in a monthly amount in order to measure MRR.

So if you have a $1,200 yearly plan, you'd just divide by 12, which would give you $100 MRR. In case you bill quarterly, you'd divide by 4.

You can also do the other way round to measure the Annual Run Rate, or simply ARR, by multiplying you MRR per 12.

Customer Lifetime Value LTV

What is LTV?

Customer Lifetime Value, usually referred as LTV (sometimes as

CLTV or CLV) measures the profit your business makes from any given customer.

The purpose of the customer lifetime value metric is to assess the financial value of each customer, or from a typical customer in case you're measuring it generally.

Customer lifetime value helps you make important business decisions about sales, marketing, product development, and customer support, such as:

- How much should I spend to acquire a customer?

- Who are my best customers? How can I offer products and services tailored for them?

- How much should I spend to service and retain a customer?

- What types of customers should sales representatives spend the most time on prospection?

How to calculate LTV?

To calculate Customer Lifetime Value we need three variables:

- ARPA (Average Revenue per Account);
- Churn Rate or Avg. Lifetime;
- Gross Margin.

The simplest way to calculate it is just multiplying ARPA versus the Customer Average Lifetime (how many months your customer stays as subscribers, on average).

LTV = ARPA * Avg. Lifetime

To calculate the Average Lifetime you can simply do:

Avg. Lifetime = 1 / Churn Rate

The best way to calculate it takes into consideration Gross Margin. To do it you should take the revenue you earn from a customer, subtract out the money spent on serving them, and see for how long they stay bringing you this profit before churning.

LTV = ARPA * % Gross Margin / % MRR Churn Rate

Improving your Customer Lifetime Value can have dramatic impacts throughout your business.

So you should always be looking for higher ARPA (customers paying you more money), higher Gross Margin (costing less to produce) and lower Churn Rate (paying you for a longer time).

Customer Profitability

Some sources may refer this calculation as CP (Customers Profitability) instead of LTV, in a way that CP represents the difference between the revenues earned from and the costs associated with the customer relationship during a specified period; and LTV represents the present value of the future cash flows attributed to the customer relationship.

Although there's no common agreement, in SaaS we tend to use LTV only.

Customer Acquisition Cost CAC

What is CAC?

Customer Acquisition Cost, or simply CAC, refers to the resources that a business must allocate (financial or otherwise) in order to acquire an additional customer.

It includes every single effort necessary to introduce your products and services to potential customers, and then convince them to buy and become active customers.

Some common sales & marketing expenses are: paid advertisement, sales and marketing staff salaries, CRM and marketing automation software licenses, events, sponsorships, gifts to customers, content production, social media and web site maintenance and more.

How to calculate CAC?

Conversion rates per sales funnel stage

One way to calculate CAC is to consider the three variables that compose it. This method allows you to go into detail and might give you good insights about your sales process cost and conversions, but can be tricky to get right.

- CPL (Cost Per Lead) (e.g. marketing costs);

- Touch cost (e.g. sales staff salaries);
- Conversion rates at each stage of the sales process.

CAC = (CPL + Touch cost per customer) * Conversion rate

Sales & Marketing expenses

An easier way to do it is sum all of your Sales & Marketing expenses and divide it by the number of customers acquired on a given period. So let's say you've spend $1,000 this month on sales & marketing and have acquired 5 news customers. Your CAC would be $200, which means you've spent $200 to bring each new customer in.

CAC = Total Sales & Marketing Expenses / # of New Customers

CAC and LTV

It's important to notice that CAC is fairly meaningless without knowing the LTV (Customer Lifetime Value). That is, the ability to monetize a customer. And every company is different, so it isn't a one-size-fits-all scenario; though generally, the more expensive the product, the higher the CAC will be.

CAC plays a major role in calculating the value of the customer to the company and the resulting return on investment (ROI) of acquisition. The calculation of customer valuation helps a company decide how much of its resources can be profitably spent on a particular customer. In general terms, it helps to decide the worth of the customer to the company.

The business challenge is to balance one against the other. Specific numbers are less important than the ratio between them. In any business model the goal is to minimize CAC while maximizing LTV. The best SaaS businesses have a LTV to CAC ratio that is higher than 3, sometimes as high as 7 or 8.

Average Revenue per Account ARPA

What is ARPA?

Average Revenue per Account (sometimes known as Average Revenue per User or per Unit), usually abbreviated to ARPA, is a measure of the revenue generated per account, typically per year or month.

You could also say that it represents the Average Revenue per Customer, but remember that a customer may have more than one account depending on your product/services characteristics.

Average revenue per account allows for the analysis of a company's revenue generation and growth at the per-unit level, which can help investors to identify which products are high or low revenue-generators.

How to calculate ARPA?

To calculate the ARPA, a standard time period must be defined. Most subscription business operates monthly but you can always calculate it yearly or quarterly according to your plans and billing options.

The total revenue generated by all customers (paying subscribers) during that period should be divided by the number total number of customers.

ARPA = MRR / Total # of Customers

New Accounts vs. Existing Accounts

There is a good practice of measuring the Average Revenue per Account separately for new customers. So instead of having an ARPA metric for all your customers, you'd have two different metrics: Average Revenue per Existing Account and Average Revenue per New Account.

That way you can have a sense of how your ARPA is evolving and how new customers are behaving if compared to existing ones. Are they more willing to accept cross selling and/or up selling? Measure it separately and you'll know.

The way of calculating it remains the same, the only different is that you're doing it with two different clusters, instead of doing it all at once.

Churn

What is Churn?

Churn is the enemy of any subscription company.

In a general definition, churn is the number or percentage of subscribers to a service that discontinue their subscription to that service in a given time period. In order for a company to expand its clients base, its growth rate (number of new customers) must exceed its churn rate (number of lost customers).

Why customers churn?

Churn is inevitable. It's impossible to guarantee that all your customers will remain being your customers forever, because churn happens for a variety of reasons. A few examples of why your customers may discontinue their subscription to your service:

- Customer out of budget/can't afford the subscription fee;
- Customer can't see/get the value our of your product;
- Your product lacks quality/features;
- Your product is good but customer service is not;
- Changed to a competitor's product;
- Your B2B customer is bankrupted;
- Your B2B customer has been acquired.

As you can see there are some events and variables that are out of your control and there's almost nothing you can do. But the good news is that – in most cases – customer churn reason is under your control, like product quality, price and customer service.

How to reduce churn?

Your challenge is to deeply understand your customers' engagement and satisfaction (using standards like Net Promoter Score) and then try to fix the problems that are under your control to prevent and reduce churn.

Churn analysis may lead to a new product roadmap to include/exclude product features, to invest in a higher quality product support or even changing your pricing model.

The best way of doing it is by making your product indispensable. It should make part of users daily workflow. Provide frequent value that they can't live without. A good strategy is to engage with your customers using email, SMS and any kind of notifications to remind them you're there for them.

Considering creating email reports showing the most important information/value your product provide to them.

Customer Churn vs. Revenue Churn

It's important to notice that Customer Churn is different from Revenue Churn. Customer Churn refers to the number of customers that have discontinued their subscription on a given period. Revenue Churn is how much those lost customers represents in revenue.

Let's say your product has a $10/mo and a $100 pricing plan.

Loosing 5 customers paying $10/mo still good if compared to loosing one single customer paying $100/mo. That's why Revenue Churn (usually referred as MRR Churn) is more important than Customer or User Churn.

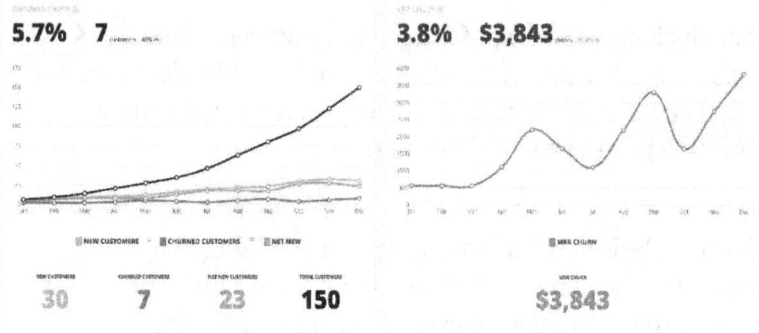

How to calculate Churn?

Customer Churn

For example, if 1 out of every 20 subscribers to your service discontinued his or her subscription every month, the churn rate for your service would be 5%. See that churn rate must be calculated for a given period, usually a year or a month.

To calculate churn, all you should do is to sum the number of customers that have discontinued their subscription on a given period. In case you sum all the churned customers in a month you'll have monthly churn, or if you sum all the customers churned in a year, you'll have yearly churn – and so on.

Churn = # of Churned Customer

Or you can calculate churn rate, representing the percentage of churned customers compared to total number of customers.

Churn = # of Churned Customer / Last Month # of Customers

Revenue Churn

Let's say that 3 customers have discontinued their subscriptions to your service on a given month. Now let's consider that the first customer was paying $10/mo, the second was paying $50/mo and the third was paying $100/mo.

Your revenue churn would be the sum of this subscription fees that will no longer come into your pockets next month, so $160.

MRR Churn = SUM (MRR of Churned Customer)

MRR Churn can also be represented in a percentage, referring to how much it represents of your total MRR.

MRR Churn % = Churned MRR / Last Month's Ending MRR

Negative Churn

Negative Churn is the dream of every SaaS/subscription entrepreneur. It happens when the expansions/up-sells/cross-sells to your current customer base exceed the revenue that you are losing because of Churn.

Getting to negative churn requires that you can do one or more of the following three things:

- **Expansions**
  Pricing model that increases according to usage growth;

- **Up-sell**
  Customers moving to a more highly featured versions;

- **Cross-sell**
  Customers to purchase additional products or services.

Keep in mind that is not easy to make negative churn happen. As David Skok says on a blog post "Why churn is critical in SaaS", in the first 12-24 months of your business it is frequently too early to figure this out. At this stage it is more important to get broad customer adoption, and that often means simple pricing that leaves something on the table for your customers.

What's an acceptable Churn Rate?

Off course the best answer for this question is "as low as possible", but we know things are not that simple.

An acceptable churn rate depends on two main factors: your target customers and your company's size/moment. Keep in mind that – if you're doing a good job – your churn rate tend to drop over the time, so this references I'm about to give you should be considered for startups around 2 years old.

Very Small Business

If you're selling to in selling to VSBs (very small business) even the most valuable services will churn at a significant rate no matter what. Unlike large startups, a VSB will have very little upsell opportunities unless the company itself grows, and many will go under or change business direction.

Small and Medium Business

If you're selling to SMBs (small and medium business) an acceptable churn rate reference would be around 3-5% monthly, but you really should target zero or negative churn. Another good reference would be < 10% annually for more healthy business.

Enterprise Level

If your targeting big corps with tickets higher than 5-digit/mo your churn rate should be under 1% and going down proportionally to your revenue growth. Enterprise SaaS is only a success if you are adding more net revenue from large-ish customers each year than you had the year before.

Earnings before interest, taxes, depreciation and amortization

What is EBITDA?

Earnings before interest, taxes, depreciation and amortization, or EBITDA, is a measure of a company's operating efficiency. EBITDA is a way to measure profits without having to consider other factors such as financing costs (interest), accounting practices (depreciation and amortization) and tax tables.

Calculating EBITDA is usually a fairly simple process and, in most cases, requires only the information on a company's income statement and/or cash flow statement.

The usage of EBITDA

Pros

EBITDA is probably the most used financial metric for startups and SaaS startups. It is well known by entrepreneurs and investors, usually used as the main indicator of operating efficiency for valuations and investment rounds.

It can also be used to compare startups against each other and against industry averages. In addition, EBITDA is a good measure of core profit trends because it eliminates some of the extraneous factors and allows a more "apples-to-apples" comparison.

While EBITDA may be a widely accepted indicator of performance, using it as a single measure of earnings or cash flow can be very misleading. In the absence of other considerations, EBITDA provides an incomplete and dangerous picture of financial health.

A common misconception is that EBITDA represents cash earnings. EBITDA is a good metric to evaluate profitability, but not cash flow. EBITDA also leaves out the cash required to fund working capital and the replacement of old equipment, which can be significant.

How to calculate EBITDA?

To calculate EBITDA, a business must know its income, expenses, interest, taxes, deprecation (the loss in value of operational assets, such as equipment) and amortization, which is expenses for intangible assets, such as patents, that are spread out over a number of years.

With those numbers in hand, the formula is:

EBITDA = Revenue − Expenses*

*Excluding taxes, interest, depreciation and amortization.

Or, more simply, it equals net income plus interest, taxes,

depreciation and amortization.

Keep in mind that EBITDA and any other financial metric should be calculated by an authorized accountant.

Custom metrics

It's important keep in mind that it's crucial that you identify your key custom metrics and measure them together with the industry standard metrics.

Imagine a company like Slack – they surely measure the number of messages exchanged between their users, channels and etc.

These custom metrics are known as "leading indicators of engaged users". The idea consists on finding a leading indicator of a user who would turn into an engaged user later on. The growth team would then focus on optimizing for that metric.

Here is how some startups thought about that indicator:

Slack

Stewart Butterfield, CEO of Slack, said that based on their experience with startups that stuck with them, any team that has exchanged 2,000 messages in its history really tried Slack.

Facebook

Chamath Palihapitiya, who used to run Facebook's growth team, said that Facebook's leading indicator of an engaged user later on was the user reaching 7 friends within 10 days of signing up.

Zynga

Nabeel Hyatt, a VC at Spark Capital, and formerly a GM at Zynga, running a 40m monthly active user game there, said that Zynga focuses on D1 retention (day 1 retention). Zynga has found that if someone comes back a day after signing up for a game, that is a leading indicator of them becoming an engaged and paying user.

Dropbox

ChenLi Wang, who runs the growth team at Dropbox, said that the leading indicator of an engaged Dropbox user is when they put at least one file in one Dropbox folder on one device.

Twitter

Josh Elman, a venture capitalist at Greylock Partners, and a former growth lead at Twitter, said that the leading indicator of engagement at Twitter was related to Facebook's metric: the user following a certain number of people, and a certain percentage of those people following the user back.

You can work to find this leading indicator in many different ways, including running advanced analytics algorithms such as linear regression – but no matter how you do – make sure to know it.

Why You Need Terms of Service

Your Terms of Service are the contract you have with your customers. A contract is an agreement between two parties to trade something for something else. You provide access to your software, and they give you money. Sounds simple.

But when they use your software, they might input their customer information, does that mean you can contact their customers? Do they get to contact your other customers, as

in a forum? Maybe you can use their picture in your advertising, like a lot of online dating sites do. And if they can use your software, does that mean they can modify it or resell it? Probably not, but do they know that? Your Terms of Service should make everything clear.

As in love, friendships, and politics, disputes arise when people don't have the same understanding about who does what and how things are supposed to be. Tom-ay-to, tomah-to. Except, when there are disagreements in business, that's when lawyers get really rich. And you don't want that, especially when it's your own money.

Imagine hiring someone to clean your house. They clean your house, and you pay them. That's a contract. But if you don't have the same understanding about how it's supposed to work, then trouble arises. Say you discover they used your detergent, mops, and a few rolls of paper towels. You thought they'd bring their own supplies. They thought you'd provide them. And they raided your fridge for their lunch, because they thought they could.

Instant misunderstanding, with its frustration and stress. This cleaning company won't be in business long, leaving a wake of frustrated ex-customers and a bad reputation, no matter how sparkling clean they left your house.

Now imagine calling another cleaning company: they tell you that they'd use your cleaning supplies. You know that upfront, before you agree to the contract. See the difference?

Say they also tell you that if they arrive and you haven't left your key in the secret hiding place, or you have a dog that's loose in the house, you'll be charged for one hour and your place won't be cleaned.

You probably prefer to deal with companies that say things like this up front. It shows they've thought of everything. It shows they care enough to point these things out. And you can tell them up front that you expect all your food to stay in the fridge.

That's what your Terms of Service do. They manage expectations. They say what happens when problems arise, to protect you from being sued when there's an outage that's not your fault (or even when it kind of is).

They are the contract that is formed when someone signs up, even when it's a free trial.

Don't worry about scaring customers off by talking about things that might go wrong.

Your sales page does the selling; your Terms of Service are the contract so it's important to have all the details and contingencies there.

The *Only* Time You Don't Need Terms of Service

You don't need to post your Terms of Service when your customers cannot sign up on your website. Sometimes it's best to meet your customers before they sign up. Some SaaS entrepreneurs want to tweak each account to customize the service.

You still need to have a contract ready for your customers, and you still need a lawyer.

This book can help you, but you'll have to do a lot more negotiating and customizing with your leads.

Check out mosaiccrm.com. It's a customized recruitment and research service for the financial services industry. But there are no Terms of Service on the site, and nowhere for new customers to sign up. Mosaic wants to meet its customers first, then negotiatespecific services and sign a contract. The contract will look a lot like Terms of Service, but it'll be slightly different for each customer.

Flavorplease helps customers who want food trucks for special events. They have Terms of Service on their site for customers, but not for food trucks. That's because not just any food truck can sign up, they have to pass a taste test. Even so, Flavorplease's Terms of Service (for customers) say that they don't endorse any truck. That means if a customer gets food poisoning, they can't sue Flavorplease. Well, they can try, but they probably won't win. Food trucks have to apply to be on the site, and they would sign contract if accepted.

You form a contract when you get a customer. When the contract is on your site and you don't meet your customers before they sign up, it's called Terms of Service.

Sometimes it's called Terms of Use. Or Terms and Conditions.

Let's get into the individual parts of your Terms of Service. Relax. Breathe. Kick off your shoes, grab a coffee and let's go.

Signing Up

Most of your customers won't read the Terms of Service when they sign up. You could have some fun with this: have the contract say that they'll agree to pay double the usual price whenever you feel like it; maybe by signing up they agree to let you crash at their mansion when you're in town. Borrow their yacht. Lend you their limo. Go ahead, dream a little. Just come back down to earth before you go to your lawyer. They will take all the fun out of it, talk to you about "misleading advertising" or "withholding important information".

Also, most of your customers won't like surprises. Best to stick to your business and how things will work in delivering your service and getting paid. Earn your own mansion,yacht and limo.

Even when you write clear, sensible Terms of Service, most customers won't read them before signing up.

So there are a few things you can do to cover your SaaS, so you don't get dragged in to a long dispute (and more lawyer's fees):

First, when they sign up, have them click on a box that says they agree to the Terms of Service. Don't allow the registration to proceed until that box is ticked.

Second, in your Terms of Service, the first paragraph (because if they click through to it, they just might read the first little bit) should say something like "by registering and using this service you are deemed to agree to these Terms of Service, and you will comply with them. If you don't agree with anything here, don't use our service." Of course you're going to get your lawyer to draft it in legal language. Make sure there are no loopholes.

Third, let them know that if they don't comply with the Terms, their account could be terminated.

[The three points above are repeated in the Appendix, items 3 and 4.]

If your customers don't quite like what's going on with your service, then they'll start reading the Terms of Service (or maybe get their lawyer to). That's when they'll find out that you can use their picture in your advertising, you can spam their inbox with ads,you can charge them extra if their data exceeds your limits. That solves that particular dispute. No lawyers involved.

If you get complaints, you might want to ease up on the spam a bit. Just because your Terms of Service say you'll do something doesn't mean you should, especially if it bothers your customers. You might lose them as customers. But these are business decisions and, again, no lawyers involved.

As your business grows, you might want to change some parts of your Terms of Service. Things change, you might add new features or new products. There might be some big court case that affects your industry or online business generally (and someone else paid lawyers for that very expensive lesson, but you can learn from it and cover your own rear end by changing your Terms of Service).

You'll have a business decision to make when you change your Terms of Service: do you give your customers notice in advance, and, if so, how much. Ask your lawyer if there's a legal requirement from your government to give notice. [Item 5 in the Appendix has this question for your lawyer.] If you can get away with no notice, put that in your Terms of Service, and tell people who sign up now that if they continue to use your service after you've changed your Terms, that signifies that they have accepted the new Terms.

Now let's decide who's in on this contract.

The Party of the First Part

Lawyers talk about "parties to a contract". It's not like there's any alcohol, loud music and wild dancing involved (unless you're in those industries, and even then, lawyers won't let it get too out of control).

The first party is you, or, more specifically, your company.

[By they way, you're incorporated, aren't you? If not, you should be. This isn't something that can wait for later. Incorporating isn't free, but it's not all that expensive. There are many benefits to operating as a corporation, but that's beyond the scope of this book.]

Somewhere in your Terms of Service you need to state your official company name,

which isn't necessarily the same as your website name or the name of your service.

Your corporation is one of the parties to the contract.

Talk to your lawyer about whether you have to put your "address for service" on your site, or in your Terms of Service, or both. An address for service is a physical location

(not a post office box number) where you can be reached.

It's good business sense for your customers to be able to reach you offline, meaning phone, fax (are they still around?) or snail mail. A physical address on your site is also reassuring to customers: it shows there's a real person behind the website.

An address for service is where a courier can show up to deliver something, and, most importantly from a legal standpoint, a place where the courts can serve you with a summons. Not a pleasant thought, but I'll bet it's necessary in your state or province when you incorporate. If someone's going to sue you, and they have to find who the website owner is and track you down that way, they're going to be even more aggressive than when they had the initial complaint. Also, it won't look good to the judge if you're trying to hide from your customers.

Now if you're an entrepreneur and just starting out, maybe you don't want your home address on the web. Maybe your parents wouldn't appreciate it, if you live with them.

Maybe you're in a condo that prohibits businesses in the apartments. You have a few options, like a friend's place, some shared office space, or your accountant's office. But don't even think about giving an address where the people there don't know you: you'd get in serious trouble if someone official couldn't get ahold of you. Talk to your lawyer if you don't want to put your home address on your website.

You might be tempted to have your address for service in another jurisdiction (meaning another state or province) that has lower taxes or is more business-friendly. It's possible, but there are costs involved and some legal technicalities. And you probably still have to pay taxes where your business operates. It's probably something to consider after your business has grown and you can afford accounting and legal advice to move your corporation. When you're just starting out, all you need is an address for service where you can be easily reached.

Your company name and address for service are items 1 and 2 in the Appendix.

The Party of the Second Part

The second party is your customer. And who is your customer? More specifically, who do you want your customer to be? In some jurisdictions, you can't make a contract with a minor, so you have to make sure your customer is old enough. Some jurisdictions allow anyone age 13 or over to sign up for something online. Your lawyer would know, and there's a reminder for you to ask in item 6 in the Appendix.

Even if your business caters to seniors, and you think no one under 18 would even think of signing up, you should still put something in your Terms of Service to make them state that they're old enough to sign up.

Also make them state that they are sane enough. Even if someone's old enough, they might be mentally incapable of entering into a contract. The courts generally decide that, if someone doesn't have the ability to make decisions, then they can't be held responsible for their end of the deal, so the agreement would be void. And you'd look like a big meanie for going after a vulnerable person, even if all your system did was

send an automatic reminder email when they missed a payment. Not that you'd take it any further: you'd just delete their account and if anyone complains you say your Terms of Service require the person to be mentally capable.

If the individual works for a corporation, you might be tempted to assume he or she is authorized to create the account, but don't assume anything when you're dealing with strangers on the internet. State it clearly: make them declare that they have authority to sign up on behalf of the corporation they represent.

And if you don't want bots signing up and taking up server space and bandwidth, state that your customer can't be a bot. [You might also want a captcha on your signup page.]

So, to answer who is your customer (item 6 in the Appendix), your Terms of Service should say they're human, of the age of majority, mentally capable, and have authority of the company they work for if they're making an account for the company.

Also, do what you can to make sure they are who they say they are: your Terms should state that they give their real names and emails. This item (7 in the Appendix) is really important. For offline contracts, you would probably meet your customer first, or at least have the opportunity to look them up to see if they're legit. Anyone who would give a false name is probably going to cause you all kinds of trouble, so it's important to be able to terminate the contract and their account as soon as you find out.

Basecamp is a project management SaaS. If you're a project manager, you've heard of it. The company that owns Basecamp is 37Signals. Here's part of their Terms of Service:

You must be 13 years or older to use this Service.

You must be a human. Accounts registered by "bots" or other automated methods are not

permitted.

You must provide your legal full name, a valid email address, and any other information

requested in order to complete the signup process.

How big is your customer?

Your customer might be a corporation with many employees. Does each employee have access to your service under one account, or does each employee need their own

account? How many individual logins can a customer have for your standard monthly

fee?

Say your SaaS helps dentists schedule patient visits. You have one customer, let's call

him Al, who has one office, and another customer, Barb, who owns and operates four

separate clinics. Does Barb need four separate accounts (one for each clinic)?

But what about a dentist, Carl, who works part-time at four clinics and wants to use your service to schedule visits? Here, he only wants one schedule (with different locations forhis appointments): it's probably not much different than Al's needs.

Unless Al has three dentists working in his clinic who each have their scheduling needs.

Maybe you'll decide to have one account per dentist, no matter where their appointments are; but a discount for other dentists in the same clinic if they're all paid at once. You have to make a business decision, and come up with a price for each account. Decide how many users (people who get access to your software) get to share one account (the business who pays you), and whether they each need their own login.

Paperless Pipeline is a SaaS for real estate brokers. The broker has the account and is the customer, but the broker can have several real estate agents working for it, as well as lawyers, land title registry people and others. The broker can allow these other people to have access to the account as what's called "authorized users", even if they're not employees of the broker. Here's how Paperless Pipeline deals with it:

Customer may allow Customer's employees, independent contractors, and agents to use the Service on behalf of Customer ("Authorized Users").

So there's one account, but lots of people using it.

As a condition to such use, Authorized Users shall abide by the terms set forth herein.

This part means that the broker can't say it wasn't his fault when one of his agents breaks the rules. Just to make it clear, there's this:

Customer shall be liable for any breach of the Agreement by any Authorized User Salesforce.com is a system for salespeople to manage their leads and sales. It allows one customer to have up to five users for their basic service. It would charge more for more than five users.

Your own decision will depend on your niche, the service you provide, the resources you'll need for each possible option, and what your customers are willing to pay. But no matter which option or service level you have, your Terms of Service need to state that your customer (the one who signs up and pays you) is responsible for all users that they allow to have access to your SaaS.

Third Parties

The third party is someone else who affects your relationship with your customer even though they're not part of the contract.

If you have a Paypal account, you and Paypal have a contract, which is completely separate from the contract you have with your customer. But you rely on Paypal to let you operate your contract with your customer. That's what makes Paypal a third party.

Your housekeeper (the one who doesn't raid your fridge) has nothing to do with your customer or your SaaS so is not a third party.

Your software has to talk to other software for you to get paid. Your Terms of Service

should state that you will share the customer's information to credit card companies,debit services, Paypal or any other company that your customer decides will process the payment. And you're not responsible for any problems with these payment services.

And their information might be governed by the Terms of Service of the third party, just to cover your SaaS. [Item 14 in the Appendix.]

If you integrate with another SaaS with an application program interface (API), that other software is a third party. Your own Terms of Service should specify that your

customer gives you permission to share his or her information with the other software package, you're not responsible for any problems with the third party, and the third party has its own Terms of Service.Also, you might change or cancel the API; your Terms of Service should state this possibility.

What You Provide

You allow your customers to access your software. It makes their own business faster,easier and maybe more fun. It saves them time, money and frustration. They love you.

You'll probably start out with a minimum viable product. You'll update your system to fix bugs or make things more efficient. You'll add new features. You might delete a feature if you see that no one's using it and it's making things awkward for your system.

There's no need to specifically define your service in the contract, but you should say that you will change the service from time to time. You'll probably publicize your changes as part of your marketing, but, still, some customers might be a bit

discombobulated because they love what you already have and don't want it to change.

Your Terms of Service need to manage expectations because you can't conquer the world without growing, and that involves changing your service as conditions change, some customers suggest improvements, or you get a great new idea that your customers love.

You might want to add new account types. Let's say you have a basic service and an enhanced service. Your basic service isn't making you much money and you'd like to create a new intermediate service and terminate your basic service. What happens to your basic customers? Well, some might buy your intermediate service, some might stop being customers, and some might demand that you continue to provide the basic service because that's what they signed up for and they have a contract, dammit, so they have the right to it, maybe under the constitution or something.

Your Terms of Service should say that you can change your service at any time, you can change the price you charge, you can terminate a tier if you want. These are business decisions and you don't want to turn them into legal issues. You'll let your customers know ahead of time, your launch will be fantastic, you'll grow your business, you'll deal gently with the few disappointed customers so they don't feel abandoned, but your SaaS is covered if your Terms say you can change the service any time.

What You Provide It On

One of the attractive benefits of SaaS is that the customer doesn't need to worry about space on their hard drive, or backing up data, or having their hard drive fry. They can get their work done anywhere they have an internet connection. But what if your system goes down, or gets hacked? Then you have three problems: a technical problem, a public relations nightmare and the possibility of customers suing you because they lost data they need to run their business. Right when they were about to sign a kazillion dollar contract too. Your Terms of Service can protect you from this last problem.

Most Terms of Service say that you will do your best to ensure the data is secure, and doesn't get mangled, leaked, stolen or hacked. That's reassuring, and it's also your job.

But you can't guarantee that everything will run the way it's supposed to. You should state clearly that you will not be liable for any lost business or other inconvenience your customer experiences when the system goes down or messes up. That's for your own protection. Your customers should understand this before they sign up and the Terms of Service are where you want to explain it. Items 10 and 12 in the Appendix have you covered.

Collecting Taxes

Make sure you collect the taxes you're supposed to. Don't try to get out of it if the law in your state or province says you have to. The government does not have a sense of humour about these things.

Then make sure your Terms of Service say that you'll collect whichever taxes you're supposed to. You don't have to list them all, because they might change. It's a question for your lawyer, in the Appendix after item 13.

How They Pay

You want to be able to charge their credit card, debit card, Paypal etc. You should treat their payment account information in the same way as you treat their names and emails:

you'll keep it confidential and use it only to collect payment. We'll talk about privacy in a later section.

You want your customers to tell you when there are any changes to their credit cards,like the account number, billing address, expiry date. Let them know in your Terms of Service. It's part of Item 7 in the Appendix.

It's a good idea to charge them at the beginning of the billing period: that way, you don't have to chase after them or give them free service. We covered this earlier too.

What happens when their payment is late? Ah, we've already covered that in the warmup exercise at the beginning of this book. You'll probably terminate their account at some point if they fail to make payments. But there are other reasons you might terminate their account, like excessive usage, doing nasty things with your software,trying to hack into your system. It's easiest to say in your Terms of Service that you can terminate their account any time you feel like it. That's item 25 in the Appendix.

Intellectual Property Rights - Your Software

Your SaaS has two major intellectual property issues. One is the intellectual property rights that you have to your software; the other is the rights your customers have to their data. The same laws apply to both situations.

There are rights attached to intellectual property. The rights can be boiled down to this:whoever has the rights can do a whole lot of stuff to make money from the intellectual property, whoever doesn't have the rights needs the rights-holder's permission to do anything to the property (like copying it, or modifying it), make any money from it, or even use it.

Copyright is one kind of intellectual property right. Others are patents (for new inventions), trademarks (think Coca-Cola or Campbell's Soup).

Copyright exists as soon as your software is written; there's no need to register it with the government (like patents). The original creator can sell all the rights and walk away with a chunk of cash, having nothing to do with it ever again. Or the creator (or whoeverbought the rights) can rent the rights, or only one right, to someone like a manufacturer or publisher (for books) in exchange for a percentage of sales (called royalties). It can be rented to only one person (called an exclusive license) or to several persons (nonexclusive license). There can be conditions on the rental, like the license is only for a year, or only for one country, or the licensee can modify it a little bit, or a lot.

Your SaaS was created by someone, and you bought the exclusive intellectual property rights to it (I hope!). So you own it.

[If you're not sure about this, check it out right now. It's really important. If your contract with your coder does not say that that he gives you and only you all rights everywhere in the world forever to the software, and he will never change his mind about it, then the courts will conclude that he owns the intellectual property rights and he was renting it to you but (a) didn't allow you to sell or rent it to someone else or (b) you're only one of the people he allows to sell or rent the software and, by the way, (c) he changed his mind and you're not allowed using his software any more. Your business could be shut down in a hurry. But developer contracts are for another book.]

Your customers need to know that they do not have any rights to your software other than what you specifically allow them to have. And you're allowing them to have the use of the software for their own business. Nothing else. In legalese, you grant your customer a license to use your software, and you're putting conditions or limitations on that license (like, they have to pay you, and all the other fun stuff in your Terms of Service).

Charitable Agents is a service that connects home buyers and sellers with real estate agents who agree to donate a portion of their sales commission to a charity of the home buyer or seller's choice. Here's what its Terms of Service say about what they're letting their software be used for:

You are granted a limited, non-exclusive, non-transferable, and revocable license to use the

Service for your personal or internal business operations use. The Company supports only those users who are accessing the Site or using the Service within the United States of America or its territories. All other users are not welcome to access the Site or use the Service.

So if you sign up with Charitable Agents, you're not the only one who can sign up, you

can't transfer your account to someone else, and they can terminate the license. Your use is limited to personal or internal business use, and only in the good ole USA.

Your Terms of Service need to clearly say that you own the intellectual property rights to your software and your customer does not. Make sure your customers understand that they can't turn around and sell or rent your software to someone else, they can't modify it, or do anything else with it that's not stated in your Terms of Service. (Item 16 in the Appendix).

Intellectual Property Rights - Your Customers' Data

Your customers will enter information into your system - their own customer lists, for example, or maybe their financial accounts. You have no control over what they enter.

They create it, so they own the intellectual property rights to it.

There are a few very good reasons for you to say in your Terms of Service that you do not own intellectual property rights to whatever your customers enter into your software:

First, to reassure them that they still control their own information. You wouldn't take that information and use it for your own purposes. Imagine if Microsoft had the rights to every document that was created using Word.

Second, to protect you from nasty things your customers might do. What if they're using your software to plot the next terrorist attack? What if it's kiddie porn? It's your customer's responsibility, not yours.

Third, to protect yourself when someone you don't even know accuses your customer of infringing his property rights. If your

Terms of Service say that you do not own the intellectual property that your customer enters, then you're covered.

There are two approaches to deal with your customer's data:

One is to state in your Terms that you don't claim any intellectual property rights to your customer's data. Here's Basecamp:

1. We claim no intellectual property rights over the material you provide to the Service. Your profile and materials uploaded remain yours.

The other is to have your customer agree to grant you a limited license to their intellectual property for the purpose of providing your service, and also your own internal customer service purposes. This is how Paperless Pipeline deals with its customer's information:

Customer shall own all right, title, and interest in and to the data that is collected by us from Customer in connection with Customer's use of the Service ("Data"). Customer grants and agrees to grant us a perpetual, non-exclusive license to use such Data (a) in order to provide Service to Customer; (b) for statistical use (provided that such data is not identifiable to Customer); and (c) as necessary to monitor and improve the Service.

Items 16 - 19 in the Appendix cover intellectual property rights.

Other Intellectual Property Issues

Some online dating sites can use your pictures for their own advertising. Would you want to use some of your customers' information for your own business purposes? If so,

you need to have it as part of your contract.

Just to be complete, you should add a clause in your Terms of Service to say that your company logo, trademarks, the look and feel of your website are your intellectual property and you do not grant permission for your customers to copy them. Now anyone who wants to make a knock-off site to fool someone into thinking it's your site probably won't be a customer, and you'd have to deal with them outside the contract you're describing in your Terms of Service. But it's good to be clear, and it only takes a minute.

Termination

All good things must come to an end. Your customer may want to end their account.

Their company is sold, they go out of business, they find something better or cheaper, they change their services, or maybe they're just not that into you any more. How do they go about terminating their account, and what happens to their data that's in your servers?

While it's never pleasant to lose a customer, you probably want to make it as simple as possible. Otherwise you'll get calls and emails from them trying to get their information out or stop you billing them. And you might get yourself a bad reputation in the industry.

Your Terms of Service should also tell your customers how much notice they need to give you to terminate. Check what the usual notice is in your industry. Sometimes it's a month, sometimes 15 days, sometimes a customer doesn't need to give notice at all.

Beta Services

One day you might want to beta test new services, or improvements to existing services. You'll want beta testers.

They know the drill - they get to test out the latest, cutting edge tech for free, and you get valuable feedback before launch. You might even get raving fans who give testimonials, tell everyone they know and become customers for life.

But maybe you'll decide you won't go ahead with the launch. Or it's more expensive than you first thought.

Your Terms of Service should clarify what happens with beta tests. You'll want to make it clear that just because someone agreed to be a beta tester, doesn't mean that they're guaranteed to get the service after launch, or ever. You can terminate the beta test any time. You'll want to give them some warning, just to be nice.

You don't need to have this section when you're just starting out. And if you have something in your Terms of Service saying you can change the Terms any time, then you can put this in when you start beta testing. But putting it in now will save going back to your lawyer later.

Standard Clauses to a Contract

There are a few things that are common to most well-written contracts, about the

contract itself.

Entire Agreement

The Terms of Service, together with the Privacy Policy, should constitute the entire agreement between you and your customer. Otherwise someone might have a unique take on something on your sales page and try to hold you responsible.

Jurisdiction You might have a customer sue you; their case may or may not be reasonable.

Sometimes people sue, or threaten to sue, just to see if you'll settle and give them some money to make it all go away. These are nuisance suits, and your Terms of Service should let you stonewall like a bureaucrat, which is cheap and fun.

But sometimes there's a real dispute. And the only thing worse than a lawsuit is a lawsuit in another country, or on another continent.

It's really important for your Terms of Service to state that any disputes would be settled by the laws of the province or state where your own business is, not your customer's.

So if a customer from the other side of the planet sues you, they would have to travel to your home city for trial.

But, if someone is infringing on your intellectual property, your own court system might not have authority over that person to make them show up for trial. You'll want to be able to sue the person wherever they are. So your Terms of Service should state that any dispute over your services (if a customer wants to sue you) will be resolved in your home state or province, and if you want to sue someone for intellectual copyright infringement, you're free to go after them wherever you feel like. Not that you're going to go around suing people; this is one of those just-in-case Terms so everyone's clear.

Limitation of Liability

YOU ACKNOWLEDGE AND AGREE THAT, TO THE MAXIMUM EXTENT PERMITTED BY LAW, THE ENTIRE RISK ARISING OUT OF YOUR ACCESS TO AND USE OF THE SITE AND SERVICES AND ANY CONTACT YOU HAVE WITH OTHER USERS OF FLAVORPLEASE WHETHER IN PERSON OR ONLINE REMAINS WITH YOU.

This one's a bit longer, yet still straightforward and complete. If anyone sues them, then neither lawyer will spend hours looking for some way around one of the examples from the list of possibilities under "including but not limited to" stuff.

One more example. Brace yourself for this one. It's brutal, but it's important.

I want you to read the item from one SaaS's Terms of Service that says you can't sue them. You've read a few others, you know you can do it.

This one, however, will be a bit of a challenge. I'm warning you, it's tough. But it's good for you, as a learning experience.

Relax, take a few deep breaths, think of the nice cup of coffee you're going to have afterwards. Or maybe the good stiff scotch. Read it, don't skip over. See how far you get before you're a quivering, broken, defeated mass crawling under your blankie in the fetal position sucking your thumb and whining "please, make it stop". Deep breath.

Ready? Here goes:

YOU AGREE TO DEFEND, INDEMNIFY, AND HOLD HARMLESS [THE COMPANY], ITS PARENTS, SUBSIDIARIES, AFFILIATES, AND THEIR RESPECTIVE MEMBERS, MANAGERS, DIRECTORS, OFFICERS, EMPLOYEES, [DEEP BREATH] STOCKHOLDERS, AGENTS AND ANY [THIRD PARTY], HARMLESS FROM AND

AGAINST ANY AND ALL CLAIMS, EXPENSES OR DAMAGES (INCLUDING ATTORNEYS' FEES), WHETHER KNOWN OR UNKNOWN, [YOU CAN DO THIS!]ARISING FROM, INCURRED AS A RESULT OF, OR IN ANY MANNER RELATED

TO (A) YOUR USE OF THE SERVICES, (B) ANY OTHER PERSON'S USE OF ANY ACCOUNT OR PIN YOU MAINTAIN, REGARDLESS OF WHETHER SUCH USE IS AUTHORIZED BY YOU, OR (C) YOUR PROMISES OR STATEMENTS MADE IN THIS AGREEMENT. [OVER HALF WAY THERE, YOU'RE DOING WELL!] YOU HEREBY AGREE TO WAIVE ALL LAWS THAT MAY LIMIT THE EFFECTIVENESS OF THE FOREGOING RELEASES. NOTWITHSTANDING THE FOREGOING, YOU SHALL NOT BE LIABLE FOR CLAIMS, [INTO THE HOME STRETCH] EXPENSES OR DAMAGES ARISING FROM THE INTENTIONAL OR GROSSLY NEGLIGENT ACTS OF [THE COMPANY] OR ITS EMPLOYEES, AGENTS, CONTRACTORS OR REPRESENTATIVES.

[YOU GOT THIS!! ALMOST THERE!] THIS INDEMNIFICATION SHALL APPLY TO THE

FULLEST EXTENT PERMITTED BY LAW AND SHALL SURVIVE TERMINATION OF

THIS AGREEMENT.

Most people just glance at text like that, and maybe that's intentional. The language in

their Terms of Service provide a clue that this company has lawyers. Maybe they're not afraid to use them.

Does that make the company arrogant? I don't think so. The company is being clear

that customers agree to not sue for anything, anywhere, any time. If they are sued, they can show the judge this Term and argue that the case should be dismissed. I don't know if it'll work in court. I can't imagine any court saying it's OK for someone to "waive all laws". But it certainly makes customers think twice about suing them.

What about your Terms of Service? If your niche is complex, if there's a lot of money at stake, if your customers are lawyered up, then you might want to have complex legalese rather than plainer grammar. But if your Terms are complex, you might spend more time on the phone or over email with customers who don't understand.

One option is to have the first few Terms of Service written in plain language and a friendly tone, with the items that customers would appreciate. Then the later clauses could be written in intimidating legalese.

APPENDIX

Please read through this, delete items that aren't applicable to your SaaS, add items you uncovered from the Cover Your SaaS game, and send it to your lawyer.

Dear Lawyer,

Please write Terms of Service and a Privacy Policy for my new software company.

My service will [give your elevator pitch]:

My customers are: [businesses? what kind? which industry?]:

1. My company name is:

2. My address for service is:

Question: can I use another address?

3. Before they can complete the registration, they'll have to click a box that says "I agree

to the Terms of Service", even if they sign up for a free trial.

4. Please read the following carefully. By signing up for [name of service], you agree to

be bound by these Terms of Service. Your account could be terminated if you fail to

comply with these Terms.

5. We reserve the right to change these Terms at any time. Your continued use of the

service will be deemed to be your acceptance of the changes.

Question: Do I have to give notice if I change the Terms of Service? How much notice?

6. You represent and warrant that

- you are of the age of majority

Question: What is the age of majority in this state/province/country?

- you are mentally capable of entering into this agreement

- you are a human. Accounts registered by bots or other automated software are

prohibited.

- If you are signing up on behalf of a business entity, you have the authority to bind that

entity.

7. You represent and warrant that all information you provide is truthful and accurate.

You agree to update your payment account information, email address and other

contact information as soon as practicable after such information changes.

8. You are responsible for all users who access the service under your account.

9. You may grant access to your account to other individuals by [what, exactly?

Establishing a separate login for each individual? Are shared logins permitted? Up to

five individuals per account?]

10. The Service is provided on an "as is" and "as available" basis.

11. We reserve the right to alter, upgrade, delete or change the Service, or any feature of the service, at any time.

1. We are not liable for any damages caused by the Service being unavailable. We are not liable for any damages caused by a breach of security.

1. The Service is billed monthly in advance and is non-refundable. We will not issue refunds or grant credits for partial months, upgrades or downgrades, or months during which you choose to not use the Service.

Question: Which taxes do I have to collect from my customers?

14. We will share your account information with payment processors for billing purposes. We are not responsible for any problems with third-party payment processors. You may be subject to the Terms of the third party.

15. We reserve the right to suspend your account if we detect excessive usage that threatens to overburden our system.

16. We reserve all intellectual property rights to our software. We grant you a limited, non-exclusive, non-transferable, revokable license to use our Service for your personal or business use.

17. We make no claim of intellectual property rights to your information.

18. You grant us a limited non-exclusive license to use your information to provide the Service, to monitor and improve the Service and for statistical purposes.

19. We reserve all rights to our logo, trademarks and the look and feel of our site.

20. We make every effort to comply with [privacy laws of your sector or regulated industry. Be specific].

21. We will use your account information for the following purposes:

- to process your payments for the Service

- to send you official notices about the Service

- to send you information we think might be of interest to you.

Question: Do I have to give them the option to unsubscribe from this?

22. We reserve the right to use your logo on our site to advertise the fact that your are a customer. You grant us a limited non-exclusive license for this purpose.

23. Your computer needs to have cookies installed in order for us to provide the

Service. We may monitor your use of the Service to improve our Service.

24. We reserve the right to remove any content you provide if it is determined in our

sole discretion to be offensive, to violate intellectual property laws, or for any reason.

1. We reserve the right to suspend or terminate your account at any time for any

reason. [Dear lawyer: I do/do not want the following list included]:

From Charitable Agents:

1. Other Restrictions. You agree to not use the Service to:

a. upload or otherwise transmit any Content or domain name that is unlawful,

threatening, abusive, harassing, tortuous, defamatory, vulgar, obscene, libellous, invasive of another's privacy, hateful, or racially, ethnically or otherwise objectionable;

b. harm or exploit minors in any way;

c. impersonate any person or entity, including, but not limited to, any the Company representative, or misrepresent your affiliation with any person or entity;

d. forge headers or otherwise manipulate identifiers in order to disguise the origin of any Content transmitted through the Service;

e. upload or otherwise transmit any Content that you do not have a right to transmit

under any law or under contractual relationships (including but not limited to inside information, proprietary and confidential information learned or disclosed

as part of employment relationships or under nondisclosure agreements);

f. upload or otherwise transmit any Content or domain name that infringes any patent, trademark, trade secret, copyright or other proprietary rights of any person;

g. remove any copyright, trademark or other proprietary notice;

h. upload or otherwise transmit any unsolicited or unauthorized advertising, promotional materials, "junk mail", "spam", "chain letters", "pyramid schemes",

or any other form of solicitation, except in those areas of the Service that may be expressly designated for such purpose;

i. upload or otherwise transmit any material that contains software viruses or any other computer code, files or programs designed to interrupt, destroy or limit the functionality of any computer software or hardware or telecommunications equipment;

j. interfere with or disrupt the Service or servers or networks connected to the Service;

k. violate any applicable law or regulation, including, but not limited to, regulations

promulgated by the U.S. Securities and Exchange Commission and any rules of any securities exchange, and laws regarding the export of technical data; (k) incite or provide instructional information about illegal activities; or

l. conduct raffles, contests, lotteries or sweepstakes, except in those areas of the Service that may be expressly designated for such purpose.

26. You may terminate your account at any time by [provide specific instructions]. Once your account is terminated, you will lose all access to the information in your account and it cannot be retrieved. Please be sure to obtain all your information before you terminate your account.

27. We will share your information with another service as part of an API. You may be subject to Terms of Service from the other provider.

28. We reserve the right to suspend or terminate your account if we detect excessive requests from the API.

29. We reserve the right to change or cancel any API at any time, with or without notice.

30. We are not responsible for any problems with the API, or any damages or

inconvenience to you caused by any problems with the API.

31. You agree that you will not:

- upload any content that violates any laws, including intellectual property laws

- access the Service to monitor its performance or for any competitive purpose

- attempt to hack into the system, disrupt or interfere with the system, servers or any

communication involving the Service.

- access the underlying code

1. We may offer beta tests of new services or features. We do not guarantee the availability of any feature or service we beta test.

33. Any disputes over this agreement will be governed by the laws of [our state or

province, our country]. We reserve the right to initiate action in any jurisdiction, including legal action, to protect our intellectual property.

34. If a court of competent jurisdiction finds one clause in this agreement to be null and

void, the remaining clauses will remain in full force and effect.

1. This Terms of Service and the Privacy Policy constitutes the entire agreement between [company name] and you and supersedes all previous agreements or promises whether written or verbal.

Privacy Policy

We collect personal information about you to provide our services and collect payment.

We will share your personal information with payment processors in order to collect payment from you.

If my company is sold, your personal information will be shared with the new owner and you will be notified.

We do not share your personal information with outside parties who are not involved in assisting us in providing our services.

We will send you emails with information about your account, your use of the service and some official notifications.

We may send you information we believe is of interest to you. you may unsubscribe from our newsletter service [provide instructions: somewhere in their account page? By notifying you? is there an unsubscribe link in each newsletter?]

We will aggregate your personal information with our other customers to monitor use of our services. We may present at industry conferences or newsletters, blogs etc. The information used in this manner will not identify you specifically.

We use cookies to save your login information and to enable certain features, and to monitor use of our service.

Your personal information is stored on servers that are not owned by us. The server provider will not share your personal information with any outside party.

Conclusions

I believe you're not reading this book by accident. You probably is running or working on a SaaS/subscription startup – and you probably already know the taste of recurring revenue.

I firmly believe we're living the subscription economy, and we're just taking off. As the venture capitalist Tomasz Tunguz said on his blog, although we may have been talking about SaaS startups for more than a decade, we're still just at the beginning.

The legacy software startups including Oracle, Microsoft, SAP and IBM control 83% of the market cap of software businesses, representing $830B in market cap. The largest SaaS company, Salesforce, is just about half the size of SAP, and Microsoft is 8x bigger.

The SaaS market is getting huge, but it stills only a piece of the subscription economy. As in any other business – metrics play a crucial part on the startups growth, and there's still a lot to learn and to be discovered.

We hope you've liked the book and that it can be truly useful in your work. Try to put things in practice and start measuring key metrics today. Start small and stay resilient.

I would love to hear your thoughts. Do you have any comments about this book? A different opinion? Feel free to reach me out.

Share your feedback:
Email us at: consulting@vardhaneharsh.com
www.vardhaneharsh.com

About the author

Vardhane Harsh
Be it writing a Marketing book at 19 or Opening a Publishing company at
20, Vardhane Harsh is a man of Entrepreneurial Excellence.As a Consultant
Marketer for Start ups,He Designs and manages Product based Campaign
Strategies , Leads Marketing Teams to their targets and Plays key roles in Client
Procurements and Brand Induction and Management. His recent new role as a
Capital Adviser has already made him popular among mid level Venture Capitalists
and Investors